I0446373

Servant Leadership in the Digital Age

SHAUN NICHOLS

Copyright © 2023 Shaun P. Nichols
All rights reserved.

Table of Contents

CHAPTER 1: INTRODUCTION

The Digital Age has ushered in an era of unprecedented technological advancement, reshaping the way we live, work, and interact. The rapid pace of innovation has not only transformed industries and economies but has also presented unique challenges for leaders navigating the complexities of this digital landscape. In this chapter, we will delve into the profound impact of the Digital Age on leadership, explore the foundational principles of servant leadership, and set the stage for our overarching thesis: the critical role of servant leadership in successfully navigating the digital complexities of the modern era.

1.1 The Digital Age: A Transformative Landscape

At the heart of the 21st century, the Digital Age has become synonymous with change, disruption, and continuous evolution. Advancements in technology, fueled by the relentless pursuit of innovation, have permeated every aspect of our personal and professional lives. From artificial intelligence and machine learning to the Internet of Things and blockchain, the Digital Age has given rise to a technologically interconnected world, bringing both opportunities and challenges.

The impact of the Digital Age extends far beyond the confines of technology itself. It has fundamentally altered the way businesses operate, reshaped the nature of work, and redefined the expectations of leaders. The traditional hierarchical structures that once defined leadership are giving way to more agile, collaborative, and adaptive models. Leaders are now tasked with navigating an environment characterized by constant change, global connectivity, and the ever-present influence of digital technologies.

1.2 Introduction to Servant Leadership Principles

Amidst the dynamic landscape of the Digital Age, servant leadership emerges as a compelling and relevant leadership philosophy. Coined by Robert K. Greenleaf in the 1970s, servant leadership emphasizes a holistic approach to leadership, where the leader's primary focus is on serving the needs of others. Rather than viewing leadership as a position of power and authority, servant leadership sees leaders as stewards of their teams and organizations, committed to the growth and well-being of those they lead.

Servant leadership is grounded in a set of principles that include empathy, humility, self-awareness, and a deep commitment to the development of others. These principles resonate with the challenges posed by the Digital Age, where agility, collaboration, and a people-centric approach are increasingly recognized as essential elements of effective leadership. As we embark on a journey through this book, we will explore how servant leadership principles can be applied to address the unique demands of the Digital Age.

1.3 Navigating Digital Complexities through Servant Leadership: A Thesis Statement

The convergence of the Digital Age and servant leadership principles forms the crux of our exploration. In this book, we contend that the application of servant leadership is not only relevant but imperative for leaders striving to navigate the intricate challenges posed by the Digital Age. Our thesis asserts that servant leadership provides a framework for leaders to authentically connect with their teams, foster collaborative environments, and lead with empathy in the face of constant technological change.

As we progress through the subsequent chapters, we will examine how servant leadership principles can be harnessed to address specific challenges inherent in the

Digital Age. From leading virtual teams to fostering innovation and navigating ethical dilemmas, servant leadership serves as a guiding philosophy that aligns with the demands of a rapidly evolving digital landscape. Through case studies, practical insights, and reflections on real-world scenarios, we will illuminate the path for leaders aspiring to thrive in the digital complexities of the 21st century.

In the chapters that follow, we will explore the historical evolution of leadership, delve deeper into the core principles of servant leadership, and examine its applicability in addressing the unique challenges and opportunities presented by the Digital Age. Join us on this journey as we uncover the synergies between servant leadership and the demands of the modern, digitally-driven world.

CHAPTER 2: THE EVOLUTION OF LEADERSHIP

2.1 A Historical Perspective on Leadership

To understand the present and anticipate the future, we must first embark on a journey through the annals of history to explore the roots and evolution of leadership. Leadership, in various forms, has been a constant companion of human civilization. From tribal chiefs and monarchs to military commanders and industrial magnates, the concept of leadership has taken on diverse manifestations across cultures and epochs.

In ancient civilizations, leadership often centered around authority and hierarchy. The ruler or chief held a position of power, making decisions that cascaded down through the social structure. Leadership was synonymous with command, and the leader's authority was unquestioned. However, as societies evolved and encountered new challenges, so too did the concept of leadership undergo transformations.

The Industrial Revolution marked a pivotal juncture in the evolution of leadership. With the rise of large-scale industrialization, organizational structures became more complex. Leaders were now required not only to command but also to manage intricate systems. The shift towards bureaucratic models of leadership introduced a more systematic and rule-based approach to organizational governance. Leaders were expected to be administrators, ensuring the smooth functioning of increasingly complex institutions.

2.2 Emergence of Digital Technologies and Their Influence on Leadership Styles

The latter half of the 20th century witnessed the advent of digital technologies that would revolutionize the very fabric of society. The rise of computers, the birth of the internet, and the proliferation of communication technologies heralded the beginning of the Digital Age. In this era of rapid technological advancement, leadership styles faced unprecedented challenges and opportunities.

Digital technologies introduced new dimensions to communication, collaboration, and information sharing. The command-and-control model of leadership, reminiscent of earlier eras, began to show signs of inadequacy in the face of dynamic, information-rich environments. Leaders had to adapt to the accelerating pace of change and the increasing interconnectedness of the world.

Leadership styles started shifting towards more participatory and collaborative models. The digital landscape demanded leaders who could navigate ambiguity, embrace innovation, and foster environments conducive to continuous learning. The emergence of knowledge-based economies emphasized the importance of intellectual capital, pushing leaders to recognize and harness the potential of their teams.

2.3 Shifting Paradigms in the Digital Era

As we stand at the crossroads of the 21st century, the Digital Age has ushered in a paradigm shift in leadership. The traditional top-down, authoritative leadership style is giving way to more inclusive and adaptive approaches. The hierarchical pyramid is being replaced by flatter structures that encourage collaboration and decentralized decision-making.

One of the key catalysts for this paradigm shift is the democratization of information. In the digital era, information is no longer confined to the upper echelons of an organization; it is accessible to everyone. Leaders are no longer just information disseminators but facilitators of knowledge sharing. This shift places a premium on leaders who can create a shared vision, inspire collaboration, and empower their teams to contribute meaningfully.

Moreover, the Digital Age has amplified the need for agility in leadership. The pace of technological change demands leaders who can swiftly adapt strategies, embrace innovation, and navigate uncertainty. The ability to lead in ambiguity has become a hallmark of effective leadership in the digital era.

The rise of remote work and virtual collaboration further underscores the evolving nature of leadership. Leaders must now manage teams dispersed across geographical boundaries, necessitating a shift from physical presence to digital connectivity. Building and maintaining relationships in virtual spaces become paramount, requiring leaders to rely on effective communication and relationship-building skills.

In the chapters that follow, we will explore how these shifting paradigms in the Digital Age align with and, at times, challenge the principles of servant leadership. We will delve into the intricacies of leading in an era defined by constant change, global connectivity, and the continuous influence of digital technologies. Join me as we navigate the contours of leadership evolution and unveil the symbiotic relationship between the Digital Age and servant leadership principles.

CHAPTER 3: UNDERSTANDING SERVANT LEADERSHIP

3.1 Definition and Key Principles of Servant Leadership

Servant leadership, a concept introduced by Robert K. Greenleaf in the 1970s, stands as a compelling alternative to traditional models of leadership. At its core, servant leadership flips the conventional hierarchy by emphasizing the leader's role as a servant first. Rather than wielding authority for its own sake, the servant leader prioritizes the well-being and development of those they lead. As we delve into the key principles of servant leadership, it becomes evident that this approach transcends mere management; it becomes a philosophy, a way of being.

Principle 1: Service to Others Servant leadership places service at its foundation. The leader's primary responsibility is to serve the needs of their team members, fostering an environment where individuals can flourish both personally and professionally. This principle challenges leaders to shift their focus from self-interest to the well-being and growth of others.

Principle 2: Empathy and Emotional Intelligence

Empathy is a cornerstone of servant leadership. Understanding the feelings and perspectives of others allows leaders to make informed and compassionate decisions. Emotional intelligence, the ability to recognize and manage one's own emotions and those of others, is a crucial aspect of this principle. Servant leaders prioritize creating a supportive and emotionally intelligent workplace.

Principle 3: Humility and Self-awareness Servant leaders exhibit humility, acknowledging their own limitations and valuing the contributions of others. This humility is coupled with a profound self-awareness that enables leaders to recognize their strengths and weaknesses. Such self-awareness fosters authenticity, as leaders lead from a place of genuine understanding of themselves and their impact on others.

Principle 4: Vision and Foresight While servant leaders prioritize the needs of their team, they also possess a clear vision for the future. This vision, coupled with foresight, enables leaders to navigate uncertainty and guide their teams toward shared goals. Servant leadership is not about abandoning strategic vision but about aligning it with the well-being of those being led.

Principle 5: Empowerment and Development A central tenet of servant leadership is the empowerment and development of others. Leaders actively seek to unlock the potential within their team members, providing the necessary support and resources for growth. The success of the leader is intrinsically tied to the success and development of the individuals under their care.

Principle 6: Building Community Servant leaders understand the importance of fostering a sense of community within the organization. They strive to create an inclusive and collaborative environment where team members feel connected and valued. Building community extends beyond the confines of the workplace, embracing a broader social responsibility.

3.2 Historical Roots and Development of Servant Leadership

While Robert K. Greenleaf is often credited with popularizing the term "servant leadership" in the modern context, the roots of this philosophy can be traced back through history and across cultures. The idea of leaders as servants, rather than rulers, has appeared in various forms throughout different epochs.

One notable historical figure often cited in discussions of servant leadership is Lao Tzu, the ancient Chinese philosopher and author of the Tao Te Ching. Lao Tzu's teachings emphasized the idea of leading by serving and the importance of humility and compassion in leadership. Similar concepts can be found in various religious and philosophical traditions, underscoring the timeless nature of servant leadership principles.

Greenleaf's formalization of the concept in the 1970s marked a pivotal moment in the development of servant leadership. Through his writings, particularly in the essay "The Servant as Leader," Greenleaf articulated a cohesive framework for a leadership style that prioritized service, empowerment, and a holistic approach to the well-being of followers. Greenleaf's work spurred further exploration and research into servant leadership, solidifying its place as a relevant and transformative leadership philosophy.

3.3 Relevance in Contemporary Leadership Contexts

In the dynamic landscape of contemporary leadership, characterized by rapid technological advancements and shifting organizational structures, servant leadership has emerged as a particularly relevant and resonant philosophy. Several factors contribute to its applicability in the modern context.

Adaptability to Change: The Digital Age is synonymous with change and uncertainty. Servant leadership, with its emphasis on flexibility, empathy, and foresight, provides a robust framework for leaders navigating the complexities of constant transformation. Leaders who embrace servant leadership principles are better equipped to lead their teams through change, fostering adaptability and resilience.

Collaborative Environments: The interconnected nature of the digital era demands leaders who can cultivate collaborative environments. Servant leaders prioritize building strong relationships, fostering open communication, and creating a sense of community within their teams. In a world where virtual collaboration is increasingly prevalent, these relational skills become indispensable.

Employee Engagement and Well-being: The well-being of employees is a critical aspect of contemporary leadership. Servant leaders recognize the importance of employee engagement, job satisfaction, and personal development. By prioritizing the needs of their team members, servant leaders contribute to a positive and fulfilling work environment, enhancing both individual and collective performance.

Ethical Leadership: The ethical dimensions of leadership are under greater scrutiny in the modern world. Servant leadership, with its emphasis on values, integrity, and a broader sense of social responsibility, aligns well with the expectations for ethical leadership. Leaders who prioritize the well-being of their teams are more likely to make ethical decisions that benefit both individuals and the broader community.

Global Leadership Challenges: In an era of globalization, leaders often find themselves navigating diverse and multicultural environments. Servant leadership, with its emphasis on empathy and cultural awareness, provides a framework for effective global leadership. Leaders who understand and appreciate the unique perspectives of individuals from different backgrounds are better positioned to lead in diverse and international contexts.

As we delve deeper into the subsequent chapters, we will explore how servant leadership can be specifically applied to address the challenges presented by the Digital Age. From leading virtual teams to fostering innovation and navigating ethical dilemmas, the principles of servant leadership serve as a guiding light for leaders aspiring to thrive in the complexities of the 21st century. Join me as we unravel the practical applications of servant leadership in the modern leadership landscape, demonstrating its enduring relevance and transformative potential.

CHAPTER 4: DIGITAL CHALLENGES IN LEADERSHIP

4.1 Identification of Challenges Posed by Digital Advancements

The Digital Age has ushered in a transformative era, marked by unprecedented technological advancements that have reshaped the way organizations operate and leaders lead. While the benefits of digital technologies are vast, they also bring forth a unique set of challenges for leaders navigating this dynamic landscape.

Pace of Technological Change: One of the primary challenges leaders face in the Digital Age is the rapid pace of technological change. Innovations such as artificial intelligence, automation, and blockchain are not only disrupting traditional industries but are also reshaping the nature of work itself. Leaders must grapple with the constant need to adapt to emerging technologies and integrate them into their organizational strategies.

Information Overload: The digital era is characterized by an abundance of information. While access to data can be a valuable asset, it also presents the challenge of information overload. Leaders must sift through vast amounts of data to make informed decisions, discerning meaningful insights from the noise. Balancing the need for data-driven decision-making with the risk of analysis paralysis is a delicate task for leaders in the digital landscape.

Cybersecurity Concerns: With the increasing reliance on digital technologies comes the escalating threat of cybersecurity breaches. Leaders must navigate the complex landscape of cybersecurity to protect their organizations from data breaches, ransomware attacks, and other malicious activities. The challenge is not only in implementing robust security measures but also in staying ahead of evolving cyber threats.

Ethical Dilemmas in Technology: The integration of technology into various aspects of business raises ethical considerations. Leaders must grapple with questions related to privacy, data ownership, and the ethical use of emerging technologies. Striking a balance between leveraging technology for innovation and ensuring ethical practices poses a significant challenge in the digital age.

4.2 Globalization, Remote Work, and Virtual Collaboration

Digital advancements have facilitated the globalization of business, enabling organizations to operate on a global scale. While this presents opportunities for growth, it also introduces unique challenges for leaders.

Global Team Management: Leading teams spread across different geographical locations and time zones requires a nuanced approach. Cultural differences, language barriers, and varying work practices add layers of complexity to team dynamics. Leaders must develop cross-cultural competencies and implement strategies that foster collaboration and cohesion in global teams.

Remote Work Challenges: The rise of remote work, accelerated by digital technologies, has become a defining feature of the modern workplace. While remote work offers flexibility and access to a broader talent pool, it also poses challenges related to communication, collaboration, and employee engagement. Leaders must navigate the complexities of managing remote teams while ensuring productivity and well-being.

Virtual Collaboration: Collaboration in virtual environments presents its own set of challenges. The absence of face-to-face interactions can hinder relationship-building and communication. Leaders must leverage digital tools effectively, promote virtual team-building activities, and create a culture of open communication to overcome the barriers of virtual collaboration.

Time Zone and Connectivity Issues: Global teams operating in different time zones face challenges related to coordination and connectivity. Leaders must implement strategies to accommodate diverse working hours, ensuring that team members can collaborate seamlessly despite geographical dispersion. The effective use of technology becomes crucial in mitigating time zone-related challenges.

4.3 Balancing Innovation and Stability

The Digital Age is characterized by a constant push for innovation and disruption. While innovation is essential for staying competitive and relevant, leaders also face the imperative of maintaining stability within their organizations.

Innovation Imperative: The rapid pace of technological change necessitates a culture of innovation within organizations. Leaders must foster environments that encourage creativity, experimentation, and the pursuit of new ideas. Embracing innovation is not only about adopting new technologies but also about instilling a mindset that values continuous improvement.

Risk Management in Innovation: While innovation is essential, it comes with inherent risks. Leaders must navigate the delicate balance between encouraging innovation and managing the associated risks. This includes anticipating potential challenges, assessing the impact of disruptive technologies, and implementing risk mitigation strategies to ensure organizational stability.

Legacy Systems and Resistance to Change: Many organizations grapple with legacy systems that may hinder innovation. Leaders must address the challenges of transitioning from traditional systems to modern, digital solutions. Resistance to change among employees is another obstacle that leaders must overcome, requiring effective change management strategies to facilitate a smooth transition.

Strategic Adaptability: The ability to adapt strategically to changing technological landscapes is a critical leadership skill. Leaders must be agile in responding to market trends, customer needs, and competitive pressures. This requires a proactive approach to scanning the external environment, identifying emerging technologies, and aligning organizational strategies accordingly.

As leaders grapple with the digital challenges outlined in this chapter, the principles of servant leadership emerge as a guiding philosophy that aligns with the demands of the Digital Age. From addressing ethical considerations in technology to fostering collaboration in global virtual teams, servant leadership provides a framework for leaders to navigate the complexities and seize the opportunities presented by digital advancements. In the chapters that follow, we will delve into the practical application of servant leadership principles to address these challenges, offering insights and strategies for leaders striving to lead effectively in the digital landscape. Join me as we explore the intersection of servant leadership and the evolving demands of the 21st-century leadership landscape.

CHAPTER 5: AUTHENTICITY IN THE DIGITAL AGE

5.1 Importance of Authentic Leadership

Authenticity is the cornerstone of effective leadership in the Digital Age. As the business landscape becomes increasingly complex and interconnected, leaders who embody authenticity are better positioned to navigate the challenges and uncertainties of the modern era. Authentic leadership is characterized by a genuine and transparent expression of one's values, beliefs, and identity, fostering trust, collaboration, and employee engagement.

Trust and Credibility: Authentic leaders inspire trust and confidence among their team members. When leaders are transparent about their intentions, decisions, and vulnerabilities, it builds credibility. Trust is the currency of effective leadership, and authenticity is the key to earning and maintaining that trust in the digital age.

Employee Engagement: Authentic leadership is closely linked to increased employee engagement. When leaders are authentic, employees feel a stronger connection to the organization and its mission. Authentic leaders create a sense of purpose and meaning, motivating team members to contribute their best efforts and ideas.

Adaptability and Resilience: Authentic leaders are comfortable with vulnerability and open to change. In a rapidly evolving digital landscape, adaptability is crucial. Authentic leaders acknowledge their own imperfections, learn from setbacks, and model resilience, creating a culture that embraces change rather than fearing it.

Organizational Culture: Authentic leadership shapes the culture of an organization. When leaders embody authenticity, it encourages employees to bring their true selves to work. This fosters a culture of openness, innovation, and collaboration, where diverse perspectives are valued and respected.

5.2 Challenges and Opportunities for Authenticity in a Digital Environment

The digital environment poses both challenges and opportunities for leaders striving to maintain authenticity. Navigating these complexities requires a nuanced understanding of the unique dynamics of digital communication and the cultivation of a leadership style that remains genuine and transparent.

Digital Communication Challenges: The absence of face-to-face interactions in digital communication channels can make it challenging for leaders to convey authenticity. Text-based communication, such as emails and instant messages, lacks the non-verbal cues that contribute to the perception of authenticity. Leaders must be mindful of the potential for misinterpretation and work to convey sincerity through digital channels.

Authenticity in the Age of Social Media: Social media platforms provide leaders with unprecedented opportunities to connect with a global audience. However, the curated nature of social media can create challenges for authenticity. Leaders must strike a balance between maintaining a professional image and authentically sharing insights, experiences, and perspectives.

Digital Visibility and Accessibility: The digital age demands leaders to be visible and accessible online. While this provides opportunities for leaders to connect with a broader audience, it also requires careful management of one's digital presence. Leaders must navigate the fine line between sharing authentic content and maintaining a professional online persona.

Balancing Privacy and Transparency: Authentic leadership involves being open and transparent, but leaders also have a right to privacy. Striking the right balance between transparency and protecting personal boundaries is a challenge in the digital age. Leaders must carefully consider what aspects of their personal and professional lives to share publicly.

5.3 Building Trust in Virtual Relationships

Trust is the bedrock of effective leadership, and in virtual relationships, where face-to-face interactions are limited, building and maintaining trust takes on added significance. Leaders must employ strategies to cultivate trust in the digital realm, fostering meaningful connections despite physical distances.

Effective Communication: Clear and consistent communication is foundational to building trust in virtual relationships. Leaders must articulate their expectations, share information openly, and ensure that team members are well-informed. Utilizing various digital communication tools, such as video conferencing and collaborative platforms, enhances the richness of communication in virtual settings.

Authenticity in Communication: Authentic leaders prioritize open and honest communication. In virtual relationships, authenticity is conveyed through written messages, video interactions, and other digital means. Leaders should strive to communicate transparently, acknowledging challenges, sharing successes, and expressing genuine care for the well-being of team members.

Building Personal Connections: Despite the digital divide, leaders can build personal connections in virtual relationships. Taking the time to learn about team members on a personal level, expressing empathy, and recognizing individual achievements contribute to the development of trust. Virtual team-building activities, informal check-ins, and digital celebrations foster a sense of connection.

Consistency and Reliability: Consistency is key to building trust in virtual relationships. Leaders must be reliable in meeting commitments, consistently communicating expectations, and providing timely feedback. Trust is eroded when there is inconsistency in leadership behavior or when promises are not upheld.

Encouraging Open Feedback: Trust is a two-way street, and leaders should actively seek and value feedback from team members. Creating a culture where open communication is encouraged, and constructive feedback is welcomed contributes to the development of trust. Leaders who demonstrate a willingness to listen and adapt based on feedback strengthen the foundation of trust in virtual relationships.

CHAPTER 6: BUILDING RELATIONSHIPS IN A VIRTUAL WORLD

6.1 Strategies for Effective Relationship-Building in Digital Spaces

As the workplace continues its digital transformation, effective relationship-building in virtual environments becomes a critical skill for leaders. The traditional methods of face-to-face interaction are no longer the primary means of connection. Instead, leaders must adapt their strategies to foster meaningful relationships within the digital realm.

Digital Communication Tools: Embracing and leveraging digital communication tools is fundamental to effective relationship-building in virtual spaces. Video conferencing platforms, messaging apps, and collaborative project management tools facilitate real-time interactions and shared experiences. Leaders should ensure that their teams are proficient in utilizing these tools to enhance communication and collaboration.

Structured Communication Plans: Establishing clear and structured communication plans is essential in virtual teams. This includes setting expectations for response times, preferred communication channels, and guidelines for effective digital communication. A well-defined communication strategy reduces ambiguity and fosters a more connected and engaged team.

Scheduled One-on-One Interactions: In the absence of spontaneous office interactions, leaders should prioritize scheduled one-on-one interactions with team members. Regular check-ins provide an opportunity for personal connection, allowing leaders to understand the individual needs and concerns of team members. These interactions contribute to building trust and rapport.

Virtual Team-building Activities: Virtual team-building activities play a crucial role in relationship-building. Leaders can organize online activities such as virtual team lunches, game nights, or collaborative projects that encourage team members to interact in a more informal and relaxed setting. These activities foster a sense of camaraderie and strengthen team bonds.

Recognition and Appreciation: Acknowledging and appreciating the contributions of team members is a powerful relationship-building strategy. Leaders should use digital platforms to publicly recognize achievements, express gratitude, and celebrate milestones. Regularly highlighting individual and team successes reinforces a positive and supportive team culture.

6.2 Overcoming Communication Barriers in Virtual Teams

Effective communication is the lifeblood of successful virtual teams. However, virtual environments introduce unique challenges that can impede communication. Overcoming these barriers requires intentional strategies and a commitment to fostering clear, open, and inclusive communication.

Clarifying Expectations: Ambiguity in expectations can lead to misunderstandings and communication breakdowns. Leaders must set clear expectations regarding tasks, deadlines, and communication norms. Clearly outlining roles and responsibilities helps team members understand their contributions and reduces the likelihood of miscommunication.

Active Listening: In virtual settings, active listening becomes even more crucial. Leaders should encourage a culture of active listening, where team members feel heard and understood. Using video conferencing tools and maintaining eye contact, even virtually, enhances the perception of attentiveness and engagement.

Written Communication Skills: In the absence of face-to-face interactions, written communication takes center stage. Leaders and team members alike must hone their written communication skills, ensuring clarity, brevity, and tone sensitivity. Emoticons, gifs, and other visual elements can add nuance to written communication.

Regular Feedback Loops: Establishing regular feedback loops is essential for maintaining a sense of connection and progress. Leaders should schedule regular team meetings, one-on-one check-ins, and feedback sessions. Providing constructive feedback and encouraging open dialogue creates a culture of continuous improvement.

Digital Etiquette and Norms: Establishing digital etiquette and norms helps mitigate misunderstandings. Leaders should communicate guidelines for virtual meetings, such as muting microphones when not speaking, using video to enhance engagement, and respecting time zones. Consistent adherence to these norms creates a more organized and effective virtual communication environment.

6.3 Fostering a Sense of Community in Remote Work Environments

The virtual nature of remote work can sometimes lead to feelings of isolation and detachment. Leaders play a pivotal role in fostering a sense of community, ensuring that team members feel connected, engaged, and part of something larger than themselves.

Virtual Coffee Breaks and Social Hours: Informal interactions are vital for building a sense of community. Leaders can organize virtual coffee breaks, social hours, or casual check-ins to create opportunities for team members to connect on a personal level. These informal gatherings mimic the spontaneous interactions that occur in traditional office settings.

Digital Collaboration Platforms: Leveraging digital collaboration platforms helps create a virtual workspace that fosters a sense of community. Platforms such as Slack, Microsoft Teams, or Asana provide spaces for team members to share ideas, collaborate on projects, and engage in ongoing conversations. These platforms serve as digital hubs for team interaction.

Celebrating Milestones and Achievements: Recognizing and celebrating milestones, both personal and professional, contributes to a positive team culture. Leaders can organize virtual celebrations for work anniversaries, project completions, or personal achievements. This not only boosts morale but also reinforces the idea that individual contributions are valued.

Employee Resource Groups: Establishing employee resource groups or affinity groups based on shared interests or identities promotes a sense of community. These groups provide a platform for team members to connect over common interests, fostering a sense of belonging and camaraderie within the organization.

Encouraging Inclusivity: In virtual environments, leaders must actively work to ensure inclusivity. This includes creating opportunities for all team members to participate in discussions, recognizing diverse perspectives, and addressing any potential feelings of exclusion. An inclusive virtual environment contributes to a stronger sense of community.

As leaders navigate the challenges and opportunities of building relationships in virtual settings, the principles of servant leadership become particularly relevant. Servant leaders, with their emphasis on empathy, active listening, and a genuine concern for the well-being of others, provide

a framework for fostering meaningful connections in the

digital age.

CHAPTER 7: SERVANT LEADERSHIP AND TEAM DYNAMICS

7.1 Applying Servant Leadership Principles to Team Dynamics

Servant leadership, with its emphasis on serving others and fostering the growth and well-being of individuals, provides a powerful framework for enhancing team dynamics in the digital age. As organizations increasingly rely on virtual teams and collaboration tools, the principles of servant leadership offer valuable guidance on how leaders can navigate the complexities of team dynamics in the modern workplace.

Individualized Support: In virtual teams, where team members may be physically distant and communication occurs primarily through digital channels, individualized support becomes paramount. Servant leaders take the time to understand the unique strengths, challenges, and aspirations of each team member. This personalized approach fosters a sense of care and support, enhancing individual well-being and overall team dynamics.

Active Listening and Empathy: Servant leaders excel in active listening and demonstrating empathy, skills that are crucial for effective team dynamics. In virtual settings, where non-verbal cues may be limited, leaders must actively seek to understand the perspectives and emotions of team members. By demonstrating genuine empathy, leaders create a culture of trust and connection within the team.

Humility and Collaboration: Servant leaders embody humility, acknowledging their own limitations and valuing the contributions of others. In virtual team dynamics, this humility is particularly important. Leaders who prioritize collaboration over authority create an environment where team members feel empowered to share ideas, contribute their expertise, and collaborate towards common goals.

Shared Decision-Making: Servant leaders involve team members in the decision-making process. In virtual teams, where collaboration may occur across time zones and geographical boundaries, shared decision-making reinforces a sense of ownership and commitment. By actively seeking input from team members, leaders tap into diverse perspectives and enhance the overall quality of decision-making.

Building a Sense of Community: The principles of servant leadership align seamlessly with the goal of building a sense of community within virtual teams. Servant leaders prioritize the well-being and development of each team member, creating an environment where individuals feel valued and connected. Building a sense of community fosters a collaborative spirit and strengthens team dynamics.

7.2 Empowering and Developing Team Members in a Digital Setting

Empowering and developing team members are central tenets of servant leadership. In the digital setting, where autonomy, skill development, and continuous learning are crucial, servant leaders play a pivotal role in creating an environment that empowers individuals to reach their full potential.

Autonomy and Trust: Servant leaders trust their team members and empower them with a degree of autonomy. In virtual teams, this trust becomes even more critical. Leaders should provide clear expectations, set goals, and then allow team members the autonomy to determine the best approach to achieving those goals. This sense of trust empowers individuals and enhances their confidence and capabilities.

Skill Development Opportunities: Servant leaders actively support the skill development of their team members. In the digital age, where the landscape is constantly evolving, leaders should identify opportunities for team members to acquire new skills and knowledge. This may involve providing access to online training, workshops, or mentorship programs that contribute to individual and collective growth.

Encouraging Innovation and Creativity: Servant leaders foster an environment that encourages innovation and creativity. In virtual teams, leaders can empower team members to explore new ideas, experiment with different approaches, and contribute to the organization's innovation agenda. Creating a culture that values and rewards creativity boosts morale and enhances the team's capacity for innovation.

Recognition and Feedback: Recognizing and providing constructive feedback are integral to servant leadership. In a digital setting, where face-to-face interactions are limited, leaders must proactively seek opportunities to acknowledge the contributions of team members. Regular feedback, both positive and constructive, helps individuals understand their impact and provides guidance for ongoing development.

Creating a Learning Culture: Servant leaders cultivate a learning culture within their teams. In the digital age, where continuous learning is a necessity, leaders can promote a culture of curiosity, experimentation, and knowledge-sharing. This may involve establishing virtual learning communities, encouraging the sharing of industry insights, and providing resources for ongoing professional development.

7.3 Cultivating a Culture of Collaboration and Shared Goals

A hallmark of servant leadership is the emphasis on collaboration and shared goals. In the digital landscape, where virtual teams often span different locations and time zones, cultivating a culture of collaboration is essential for fostering cohesive and high-performing teams.

Shared Vision and Purpose: Servant leaders articulate a compelling vision and purpose that aligns with the values and aspirations of the team. In virtual teams, where individuals may be physically distant, creating a shared vision becomes a unifying force. Leaders should communicate a clear and inspiring purpose that motivates team members and provides a sense of direction.

Promoting Open Communication: Open and transparent communication is fundamental to collaboration. In virtual teams, leaders must prioritize clear and regular communication, leveraging digital channels effectively. Creating a culture where team members feel comfortable expressing their thoughts, ideas, and concerns fosters a sense of openness and strengthens collaboration.

Collaborative Tools and Technologies: Servant leaders leverage collaborative tools and technologies to enhance team interaction. In the digital age, a wide array of tools, such as video conferencing, project management platforms, and virtual whiteboards, facilitate real-time collaboration. Leaders should ensure that their teams are equipped with the right tools to streamline communication and project workflows.

Encouraging Cross-functional Collaboration: Servant leaders recognize the value of cross-functional collaboration. In virtual teams, where diverse skills and expertise may be dispersed across different roles and locations, leaders should actively encourage collaboration across functions. This collaborative approach fosters innovation, problem-solving, and a holistic perspective on organizational goals.

Celebrating Team Achievements: Servant leaders celebrate team achievements and milestones. In virtual teams, where physical proximity may be lacking, leaders should go the extra mile to acknowledge and celebrate successes. This may involve virtual celebrations, recognition ceremonies, or other creative ways of expressing appreciation for the collective efforts of the team.

CHAPTER 8: EMOTIONAL INTELLIGENCE IN DIGITAL LEADERSHIP

8.1 The Role of Emotional Intelligence in Leadership

In the ever-evolving landscape of digital leadership, emotional intelligence stands out as a critical attribute that transcends technological advancements. Emotional intelligence, often abbreviated as EI or EQ, refers to the ability to recognize, understand, and manage one's own emotions and the emotions of others. In the digital era, where virtual interactions often replace face-to-face communication, the role of emotional intelligence becomes even more pronounced.

Self-Awareness: At the core of emotional intelligence is self-awareness, the ability to recognize and understand one's own emotions. In leadership, self-awareness empowers individuals to navigate challenges with composure, make informed decisions, and build authentic connections with others. In the digital realm, where the nuances of in-person interactions may be absent, self-awareness becomes a guiding force for effective leadership.

Self-Regulation: Emotional intelligence equips leaders with the capacity for self-regulation, the ability to manage and control their emotional responses. In the digital age, where virtual communication can sometimes lack the immediate feedback of face-to-face interactions, leaders with strong self-regulation skills can maintain a positive and constructive leadership presence.

Empathy: Empathy, the ability to understand and share the feelings of others, is a cornerstone of effective leadership. In the digital landscape, where physical distance can create a sense of isolation, leaders who demonstrate empathy foster a connected and supportive team culture. Virtual teams benefit immensely from leaders who understand and respond to the emotional needs of team members.

Social Skills: Emotional intelligence encompasses social skills, including effective communication, collaboration, and relationship-building. In the digital workplace, where written communication often replaces verbal cues, leaders with strong social skills can navigate virtual interactions with finesse. These skills are particularly vital for fostering a positive team culture and maintaining strong interpersonal connections.

Motivation: Emotional intelligence contributes to intrinsic motivation, the drive to achieve goals and excel in one's endeavors. Leaders with high emotional intelligence inspire and motivate their teams, even in virtual settings. Motivated teams are more likely to overcome challenges, innovate, and collaborate effectively, contributing to the overall success of the organization.

8.2 Recognizing and Managing Emotions in Virtual Teams

In the absence of physical proximity and face-to-face interactions, recognizing and managing emotions in virtual teams become paramount. Digital leaders who excel in emotional intelligence can create a virtual environment that supports the emotional well-being of team members and enhances overall team performance.

Recognizing Emotional Cues in Written Communication: In virtual teams, much of the communication occurs through written channels such as emails, chat messages, and collaborative documents. Leaders with strong emotional intelligence can recognize emotional cues embedded in written communication, such as tone, choice of words, and overall sentiment. This awareness enables leaders to address emotions effectively and prevent potential misunderstandings.

Facilitating Emotional Expression in Virtual Settings:
Creating avenues for team members to express their
emotions in virtual settings is crucial for building a
supportive team culture. Leaders can leverage virtual
meetings, video conferencing, and collaborative platforms
to provide opportunities for team members to share their
thoughts, concerns, and successes. Facilitating emotional
expression fosters a sense of connection and openness
within the team.

Effective Use of Video Conferencing: While virtual
communication often relies on text-based platforms, video
conferencing provides an opportunity for more nuanced
communication. Leaders with emotional intelligence
recognize the value of visual cues, facial expressions, and
body language in understanding the emotional states of
team members. Incorporating video conferencing into
virtual interactions enhances the emotional richness of
communication.

Addressing Emotional Challenges Promptly: In virtual teams, addressing emotional challenges promptly is essential to prevent the escalation of issues. Leaders with strong emotional intelligence can recognize when team members are experiencing difficulties or emotional distress. Prompt and empathetic responses, whether through private conversations or team discussions, contribute to resolving issues and maintaining a positive team dynamic.

Building Trust Through Consistency: Trust is a foundational element of successful virtual teams. Consistency in leadership behavior, communication, and decision-making builds trust among team members. Leaders with high emotional intelligence understand the impact of their actions on trust and work consistently to foster an environment where team members feel secure and valued.

8.3 Enhancing Interpersonal Skills in the Digital Workplace

Interpersonal skills, the ability to interact and communicate effectively with others, are central to successful leadership in the digital workplace. Digital leaders with strong interpersonal skills can navigate virtual interactions, build meaningful relationships, and create a positive team culture. The application of emotional intelligence enhances these interpersonal skills in the following ways:

Active Listening in Virtual Conversations: Active listening is a foundational interpersonal skill that becomes even more critical in virtual settings. Leaders with strong emotional intelligence practice active listening during virtual conversations, ensuring that they fully understand the perspectives and concerns of team members. This skill contributes to effective communication and builds trust within the team.

Clear and Transparent Communication: Interpersonal skills are expressed through clear and transparent communication. In the digital workplace, where written communication is prevalent, leaders with strong interpersonal skills ensure that their messages are concise, easily understood, and aligned with the needs of the team. Clear communication reduces the likelihood of misunderstandings and promotes a positive team environment.

Facilitating Collaborative Decision-Making: Leaders with strong interpersonal skills facilitate collaborative decision-making processes. In virtual teams, where diverse perspectives may be less immediately apparent, leaders must actively seek input, encourage discussions, and ensure that decisions reflect the collective insights of the team. Collaborative decision-making enhances team engagement and commitment.

Conflict Resolution and Mediation: Interpersonal conflicts can arise in any workplace, and virtual teams are no exception. Leaders with strong emotional intelligence and interpersonal skills can navigate conflicts effectively. They approach conflicts with empathy, seek to understand the underlying issues, and facilitate constructive conversations to reach resolutions. Skilful conflict resolution maintains team cohesion and morale.

Building Rapport in Virtual Environments: Building rapport is a nuanced interpersonal skill that contributes to positive team dynamics. In virtual environments, leaders with strong interpersonal skills find creative ways to build rapport, such as incorporating informal interactions into virtual meetings, recognizing individual achievements, and creating opportunities for team members to connect on a personal level.

CHAPTER 9: NAVIGATING CHANGE IN THE DIGITAL LANDSCAPE

9.1 Adapting Servant Leadership to Guide Teams Through Digital Transformation

In the fast-paced and ever-evolving digital landscape, change is not just inevitable; it is a constant. Organizations that thrive in the digital era recognize the need for effective leadership to navigate change successfully. Servant leadership, with its focus on serving others and fostering individual growth, is particularly well-suited to guide teams through the challenges and opportunities of digital transformation.

Understanding the Human Impact of Change: One of the key principles of servant leadership is a deep understanding of the human aspect of organizational dynamics. In the context of digital transformation, this means recognizing that change affects individuals on a personal and professional level. Servant leaders empathize with the concerns and uncertainties that team members may experience during periods of change, fostering an environment where the human side of transformation is acknowledged and addressed.

Clear Communication and Transparency: Servant leaders excel in clear communication and transparency, essential elements when guiding teams through digital transformation. Digital change often involves new technologies, processes, and ways of working. Leaders must communicate the reasons for change, the expected outcomes, and the impact on individuals with transparency. Providing a clear roadmap and being open to questions and concerns build trust and confidence within the team.

Empowering and Involving Team Members: Digital transformation is not a top-down process; it thrives on the active involvement of team members. Servant leaders empower their teams by involving them in the change process. This may include seeking input on digital strategies, encouraging innovation, and providing opportunities for team members to contribute to the decision-making process. Empowered teams are more likely to embrace and champion change.

Continuous Learning and Adaptability: Servant leaders foster a culture of continuous learning and adaptability, qualities that are essential in the digital landscape. Digital transformation often requires acquiring new skills, adopting emerging technologies, and adapting to evolving industry trends. Leaders who prioritize learning and demonstrate adaptability set the tone for a team that is open to change and resilient in the face of uncertainty.

Individualized Support During Transition: Change can be a challenging and disruptive experience for individuals.

Servant leaders provide individualized support during periods of transition. This may involve recognizing and addressing the unique needs of team members, offering mentorship, or providing resources for skill development. Individualized support contributes to a positive and supportive environment that facilitates successful adaptation to change.

9.2 Strategies for Leading Change in a Dynamic Environment

Leading change in a dynamic digital environment requires strategic thinking, effective communication, and the ability to navigate uncertainty. Servant leaders, with their focus on the well-being and growth of individuals, can employ specific strategies to guide teams through the complexities of change in the digital landscape.

Create a Compelling Vision: A compelling vision is a driving force behind successful change initiatives. Servant leaders work collaboratively with their teams to create a vision that aligns with the organization's goals and values. The vision provides a clear direction for the change, inspiring and motivating team members to actively participate in the transformation journey.

Communicate Purpose and Benefits: Change can be met with resistance if team members do not understand the purpose and benefits. Servant leaders communicate the overarching purpose of the change and articulate how it aligns with the organization's mission. Emphasizing the benefits of the change, both for the organization and individual team members, creates a sense of purpose and clarity.

Establish a Change Roadmap: A well-defined roadmap is essential for navigating change in a dynamic environment. Servant leaders collaborate with their teams to establish a detailed plan that outlines the stages of the change process, milestones, and key responsibilities. A structured roadmap provides a sense of direction, reduces uncertainty, and fosters a proactive approach to change.

Encourage Collaboration and Innovation: Change often involves exploring new ideas and innovative approaches. Servant leaders foster a collaborative culture where team members feel empowered to contribute their insights and suggestions. Encouraging innovation not only enhances the quality of change initiatives but also instills a sense of ownership and engagement among team members.

Provide Resources and Training: Digital transformation frequently requires acquiring new skills and knowledge. Servant leaders ensure that team members have access to the resources and training necessary for successful adaptation. This may include investing in training programs, providing access to educational materials, and offering mentorship to support skill development.

9.3 Overcoming Resistance to Digital Change

Resistance to change is a natural human response, particularly in the context of digital transformation where uncertainty and unfamiliarity can breed apprehension. Servant leaders approach resistance with empathy, understanding, and proactive strategies to overcome resistance and foster a culture that embraces change.

Understand the Root Causes of Resistance: Servant leaders seek to understand the root causes of resistance rather than dismissing it outright. Resistance may stem from fear of the unknown, concerns about job security, or a lack of understanding about the benefits of change. By identifying the underlying reasons for resistance, leaders can tailor their approach to address specific concerns.

Communicate Openly and Transparently: Open and transparent communication is a powerful tool for overcoming resistance. Servant leaders communicate openly about the reasons for change, the expected outcomes, and the potential challenges. Transparency builds trust and helps alleviate concerns, creating a more supportive environment for team members to embrace the change.

Involve Team Members in Decision-Making: Involving team members in decision-making processes empowers them and reduces resistance. Servant leaders seek input from their teams, encouraging participation in decisions related to the change. When individuals feel that their opinions are valued and considered, they are more likely to support and actively contribute to the change initiative.

Provide Adequate Support and Resources: Resistance often arises when individuals feel ill-equipped to handle the challenges of change. Servant leaders provide the necessary support and resources to help team members navigate the transition. This may include training programs, mentorship, or access to external expertise. Adequate support mitigates concerns and builds confidence in the team's ability to adapt.

Celebrate Small Wins and Milestones: Recognizing and celebrating small wins and milestones is crucial for overcoming resistance and maintaining momentum. Servant leaders acknowledge the efforts and achievements of their teams throughout the change.

CHAPTER 10: THE ETHICS OF DIGITAL LEADERSHIP

10.1 Ethical Considerations in the Digital Age

In the rapidly evolving landscape of the digital age, ethical considerations have become increasingly complex and prominent. Digital leaders are faced with a myriad of ethical challenges ranging from data privacy and cybersecurity to the ethical implications of artificial intelligence (AI) and automation. Navigating these ethical considerations requires a deep understanding of the values that underpin responsible digital leadership.

Data Privacy and Security: The digital age has ushered in an era of unprecedented data generation, collection, and utilization. Digital leaders must grapple with ethical considerations surrounding data privacy and security. Respect for user privacy, transparent data practices, and robust cybersecurity measures are integral to ethical digital leadership. Leaders must ensure that data is collected and used responsibly, with a commitment to protecting individuals' privacy.

Artificial Intelligence and Automation: As organizations embrace AI and automation, ethical dilemmas emerge regarding their impact on employment, decision-making, and societal well-being. Digital leaders must consider the ethical implications of deploying AI systems, including issues related to bias, transparency, and accountability. Ethical digital leadership involves striking a balance between technological innovation and ensuring that AI and automation align with ethical principles.

Digital Inclusion and Accessibility: Ethical digital leaders recognize the importance of digital inclusion and accessibility. As digital technologies become integral to various aspects of life, leaders must ensure that their initiatives are accessible to all individuals, regardless of abilities or socioeconomic status. Digital inclusion goes beyond technological considerations; it embodies a commitment to creating equitable opportunities and addressing the digital divide.

Cybersecurity and Threat Mitigation: With the increasing prevalence of cyber threats and attacks, ethical digital leadership requires a proactive approach to cybersecurity. Leaders must prioritize the protection of organizational and user data, implement robust security measures, and stay vigilant against emerging threats. Ethical considerations extend to how organizations respond to and mitigate the impact of cybersecurity incidents on individuals and stakeholders.

Social Media and Online Influence: The ethical use of social media and online influence is a critical consideration for digital leaders. In an era of information abundance, leaders must be mindful of the impact of their online presence, communications, and influence on public opinion. Ethical digital leadership involves promoting authenticity, transparency, and responsible communication in the digital realm.

10.2 Balancing Innovation with Ethical Decision-Making

Innovation is a driving force in the digital age, fueling progress, efficiency, and competitive advantage. However, ethical decision-making must be at the forefront of digital leadership to ensure that innovation aligns with societal values, legal standards, and organizational principles.

Ethical Frameworks for Innovation: Ethical digital leaders adopt frameworks that guide innovation within ethical boundaries. These frameworks may include principles such as fairness, transparency, accountability, and a commitment to societal well-being. Leaders should proactively integrate ethical considerations into the innovation process, conducting ethical impact assessments to evaluate the potential consequences of new technologies.

Responsible AI and Machine Learning: Artificial intelligence and machine learning technologies present unique ethical challenges, including bias in algorithms, unintended consequences, and the ethical use of AI in decision-making. Ethical digital leaders prioritize responsible AI practices, addressing bias, ensuring transparency in algorithmic decision-making, and establishing mechanisms for accountability. They also advocate for ethical guidelines and industry standards in the development and deployment of AI technologies.

Sustainable Innovation: Ethical digital leadership extends to the sustainability of innovation. Leaders must consider the environmental impact of digital technologies and initiatives, adopting practices that minimize carbon footprints and promote sustainable development. Balancing innovation with environmental responsibility aligns with broader ethical considerations related to corporate social responsibility and global sustainability goals.

Stakeholder Engagement and Co-Creation: Ethical digital leaders engage stakeholders, including employees, customers, and the wider community, in the innovation process. Co-creation involves collaborating with diverse stakeholders to gather insights, incorporate diverse perspectives, and ensure that innovation serves the needs and values of the broader community. Inclusivity in the innovation process fosters ethical decision-making and creates solutions that benefit a diverse range of stakeholders.

Continuous Ethical Evaluation: Innovation is an ongoing process, and ethical digital leaders recognize the need for continuous ethical evaluation. As technologies evolve and new challenges emerge, leaders should regularly assess the ethical implications of existing practices and adapt their strategies accordingly. A commitment to ongoing ethical evaluation demonstrates a proactive approach to responsible innovation.

10.3 The Impact of Digital Leadership on Organizational Values

Digital leadership not only influences technological strategies but also plays a pivotal role in shaping organizational values. The ethical choices made by digital leaders have a profound impact on the culture, reputation, and long-term sustainability of the organization.

Culture of Integrity and Trust: Ethical digital leaders contribute to a culture of integrity and trust within the organization. By consistently making ethical decisions and upholding ethical standards, leaders set the tone for an organizational culture where trust is nurtured, and employees feel confident in the ethical principles guiding their work. This, in turn, enhances employee morale, engagement, and commitment to shared values.

Reputation and Brand Identity: Ethical digital leadership has a direct impact on an organization's reputation and brand identity. Unethical behavior, data breaches, or disregard for privacy can tarnish an organization's image, eroding the trust of customers, partners, and stakeholders. Conversely, organizations led by ethical digital leaders are more likely to build a positive reputation and foster brand loyalty.

Employee Morale and Well-Being: The ethical decisions of digital leaders influence employee morale and well-being. When leaders prioritize ethical considerations, employees are more likely to feel a sense of purpose, alignment with organizational values, and pride in their work. Ethical leadership contributes to a positive work environment, where employees feel valued, supported, and motivated to contribute to the organization's success.

Organizational Agility and Resilience: Ethical digital leadership enhances organizational agility and resilience. Organizations that prioritize ethical decision-making are better equipped to navigate challenges, adapt to changing circumstances, and maintain the trust of stakeholders. Ethical considerations are integral to building a resilient organizational culture that can withstand disruptions and emerge stronger from adversity.

Long-Term Sustainability: The impact of digital leadership on organizational values extends to long-term sustainability. Ethical organizations are better positioned for sustained success, as they foster enduring relationships with customers, partners, and the wider community. Ethical digital leaders recognize that sustainable success goes beyond immediate gains and requires a commitment to ethical practices that align with the organization's core

values.

CHAPTER 11: INNOVATION AND CREATIVITY IN SERVANT LEADERSHIP

11.1 Fostering Innovation through Servant Leadership Principles

Innovation is the lifeblood of organizations seeking to thrive in the dynamic landscape of the digital age. Servant leadership, with its emphasis on empowerment, collaboration, and a deep understanding of individual needs, provides a fertile ground for fostering innovation. In this chapter, we explore how servant leadership principles can serve as catalysts for innovation and propel organizations toward a future of sustained growth and relevance.

Empowering Teams to Innovate: Servant leaders empower their teams to innovate by providing them with the autonomy and support needed to explore new ideas and solutions. By decentralizing decision-making and encouraging a culture of experimentation, servant leaders create an environment where team members feel empowered to take risks, challenge the status quo, and contribute to the organization's innovation agenda.

Creating a Culture of Curiosity: Servant leaders cultivate a culture of curiosity within their teams, encouraging individuals to ask questions, explore possibilities, and seek innovative solutions. By fostering a mindset that values learning and inquiry, leaders inspire team members to look beyond the obvious and discover new approaches to challenges. A culture of curiosity is essential for unlocking the creative potential of individuals and teams.

Facilitating Cross-Functional Collaboration: Servant leaders recognize the value of cross-functional collaboration in driving innovation. By breaking down silos and promoting collaboration across departments and disciplines, leaders ensure that diverse perspectives and expertise are brought to the innovation process. Cross-functional collaboration fosters a rich exchange of ideas, leading to holistic and innovative solutions to complex problems.

Supporting Intrapreneurship: Intrapreneurship, the practice of cultivating an entrepreneurial spirit within an organization, is a powerful driver of innovation. Servant leaders support intrapreneurship by providing resources, mentorship, and a conducive environment for individuals to pursue innovative projects within the organization. By recognizing and nurturing the entrepreneurial aspirations of team members, leaders stimulate a culture of innovation from within.

Celebrating and Learning from Failure: Servant leaders view failure not as an endpoint but as a valuable part of the innovation journey. By creating a safe space where failure is acknowledged, analyzed, and learned from, leaders encourage a culture of resilience and continuous improvement. Celebrating lessons learned from failures fosters an environment where individuals are more willing to take calculated risks and push the boundaries of innovation.

11.2 Encouraging Creativity in a Digital Workplace

In a digital workplace where virtual collaboration and remote interactions prevail, fostering creativity becomes a nuanced challenge. Servant leaders, with their focus on individual development and relationship-building, are well-positioned to encourage creativity in the digital realm. Let's explore how servant leadership principles can nurture a culture of creativity, even in virtual environments.

Providing Autonomy and Flexibility: Creativity thrives in an environment that allows individuals the autonomy to explore their ideas and the flexibility to experiment with different approaches. Servant leaders, even in virtual settings, provide autonomy by trusting team members to manage their work and encouraging flexibility in how tasks are approached. This autonomy fosters a sense of ownership and empowerment, key ingredients for unlocking creativity.

Emphasizing Active Listening: Active listening is a fundamental servant leadership principle that plays a crucial role in encouraging creativity. In virtual interactions, where non-verbal cues may be limited, leaders must be especially attentive to verbal communication and actively seek to understand the perspectives and ideas shared by team members. By demonstrating genuine interest and curiosity, leaders create a supportive environment for creative expression.

Creating Virtual Spaces for Idea Exchange: Servant leaders leverage digital tools to create virtual spaces for idea exchange and collaboration. Whether through video conferences, collaboration platforms, or virtual brainstorming sessions, leaders facilitate opportunities for team members to share and build upon each other's ideas. Virtual spaces for idea exchange foster a sense of connection and collaborative creativity.

Encouraging Diverse Perspectives: Creativity flourishes when diverse perspectives come together. Servant leaders actively encourage diversity in thought and perspective within their teams, recognizing that varied experiences and backgrounds contribute to a richer pool of ideas. In the digital workplace, leaders use inclusive communication strategies to ensure that all team members feel heard and valued, fostering a culture of creative collaboration.

Providing Time and Resources for Creative Pursuits: Servant leaders understand the importance of dedicating time and resources to creative pursuits. In the digital age, where work may extend beyond traditional office hours, leaders actively promote a healthy work-life balance. By providing dedicated time for creative exploration and acknowledging the value of personal interests, leaders contribute to a work environment that nurtures and sustains creativity.

11.3 Leveraging Technology for Organizational Growth

Digital leaders face the dual challenge of leveraging technology to drive organizational growth while ensuring that the human element is not lost in the process. Servant leadership principles provide a balanced approach, emphasizing the responsible use of technology to enhance organizational capabilities and foster sustainable growth.

Strategic Adoption of Technology: Servant leaders strategically adopt technology to enhance organizational capabilities and drive growth. Whether through the implementation of innovative tools, digital platforms, or emerging technologies, leaders ensure that technology aligns with the organization's strategic objectives. The strategic adoption of technology is guided by a deep understanding of how it can empower individuals, improve processes, and contribute to overall organizational effectiveness.

Digital Transformation with a Human-Centric Approach: Digital transformation, while often technology-driven, is fundamentally about people. Servant leaders approach digital transformation with a human-centric perspective, considering the impact on individuals and the organization's culture. They actively involve employees in the transformation process, provide the necessary training and support, and communicate transparently about the changes. This human-centric approach ensures that technology enhances, rather than replaces, the human experience within the organization.

Facilitating Remote Collaboration and Communication: In the digital workplace, where remote collaboration is the norm, servant leaders leverage technology to facilitate seamless communication and collaboration. Video conferencing tools, collaboration platforms, and project management software become integral to virtual teamwork. Servant leaders ensure that these technologies enhance communication, support effective collaboration, and contribute to the overall well-being of team members.

Data-Driven Decision-Making: Servant leaders harness the power of data for informed decision-making. Through data analytics and business intelligence tools, leaders gain valuable insights into organizational performance, customer behavior, and market trends. Data-driven decision-making enhances the organization's ability to adapt to changing circumstances, identify growth opportunities, and optimize strategies for long-term success.

Investing in Employee Development through Technology: Technology is not only a tool for organizational growth but also a means to invest in employee development. Servant leaders leverage online learning platforms, webinars, and digital resources to provide continuous learning opportunities for their teams. By facilitating skill development and professional growth through technology, leaders empower individuals to contribute more effectively to the organization's growth trajectory.

As we explore the intersection of innovation, creativity, and technology within the framework of servant leadership, it becomes clear that these principles are not only compatible but mutually reinforcing. Servant leaders, by fostering a culture of empowerment, curiosity, and human-centric values, create an environment where innovation and technology contribute synergistically to organizational growth.

CHAPTER 12: SERVANT LEADERSHIP IN GLOBALIZED WORK ENVIRONMENTS

12.1 Leading Diverse and Multicultural Teams

In the globalized work environments of the digital age, leaders are faced with the challenge and opportunity of leading diverse and multicultural teams. The richness of diverse perspectives can contribute to innovation and creativity, but effective leadership is essential to harness the potential of diversity. Servant leadership principles provide a guiding framework for leading diverse teams with empathy, inclusivity, and a deep understanding of individual and cultural differences.

Cultural Intelligence in Leadership: Cultural intelligence, or the ability to navigate and work effectively across different cultural contexts, is a cornerstone of leading diverse teams. Servant leaders actively cultivate cultural intelligence by seeking to understand the cultural backgrounds, values, and communication styles of team members. This understanding allows leaders to adapt their approach, communicate effectively, and build strong relationships with individuals from diverse cultural backgrounds.

Promoting Inclusivity: Inclusivity is a key aspect of servant leadership, and it becomes even more critical in globalized work environments. Servant leaders actively promote inclusivity by creating an environment where every team member, regardless of their cultural background, feels valued, heard, and included. This involves recognizing and celebrating diverse perspectives, providing equal opportunities for contribution, and fostering a sense of belonging within the team.

Effective Communication in Multicultural Teams: Communication is at the heart of successful leadership in multicultural teams. Servant leaders prioritize effective communication by considering the linguistic and cultural nuances that may influence understanding. This involves clear and transparent communication, active listening, and the use of diverse communication channels to accommodate different preferences and cultural norms.

Building Trust Across Cultures: Trust is the foundation of any successful team, and building trust across cultures requires intentional effort. Servant leaders understand that trust is established through consistency, reliability, and genuine concern for the well-being of team members. By demonstrating trustworthiness and fostering an environment of trust, leaders create a cohesive and collaborative multicultural team.

Conflict Resolution in Diverse Teams: In multicultural teams, differences in communication styles, expectations, and perspectives can lead to conflicts. Servant leaders approach conflict resolution with cultural sensitivity, acknowledging and addressing the underlying cultural factors that may contribute to conflicts. Through open communication, mediation, and a commitment to understanding diverse viewpoints, leaders can navigate conflicts effectively and maintain a positive team dynamic.

12.2 Adapting Servant Leadership to Different Cultural Contexts

Servant leadership is not a one-size-fits-all approach; it requires adaptability to different cultural contexts. As leaders navigate globalized work environments, understanding and adapting servant leadership principles to diverse cultural norms and expectations is essential for building trust and fostering effective collaboration.

Cultural Sensitivity in Leadership Practices: Cultural sensitivity involves an awareness of and respect for the cultural norms and practices of team members. Servant leaders adapt their leadership practices to align with cultural expectations, whether it's in the approach to decision-making, communication styles, or the expression of authority. By demonstrating cultural sensitivity, leaders enhance their effectiveness in different cultural contexts.

Flexibility in Leadership Styles: Servant leaders embrace flexibility in their leadership styles, recognizing that different cultural contexts may require different approaches. Some cultures may value a more hierarchical leadership style, while others may emphasize collaboration and shared decision-making. Servant leaders adapt their leadership styles to accommodate cultural preferences, creating a harmonious and effective working environment.

Understanding Cultural Differences in Motivation: Motivational factors vary across cultures, and servant leaders take the time to understand the cultural nuances of motivation within their teams. Whether it's recognizing the importance of individual recognition, team achievement, or personal growth, leaders tailor their motivational strategies to resonate with the cultural values and expectations of team members.

Navigating Power Distance and Authority: Power distance, or the extent to which individuals in a culture accept hierarchical authority, is a significant cultural dimension. Servant leaders navigate power distance by understanding and respecting cultural attitudes toward authority. In some cultures, a more egalitarian leadership approach may be preferred, while in others, a more hierarchical structure may be expected. Adapting to these cultural expectations fosters a leadership style that resonates with team members.

Cross-Cultural Team Building: Building cohesive teams across cultures requires intentional efforts from servant leaders. Leaders facilitate cross-cultural team building by organizing activities that promote understanding and collaboration among team members. This may include virtual team-building exercises, cross-cultural training sessions, and initiatives that celebrate the diversity within the team. Cross-cultural team building strengthens relationships and enhances the collective effectiveness of the team.

12.3 Addressing the Challenges of Leading Global Teams in the Digital Age

Leading global teams in the digital age presents unique challenges, from overcoming time zone differences to navigating cultural diversity through virtual communication. Servant leaders, with their focus on empathy, collaboration, and individual development, are well-equipped to address these challenges and foster a sense of unity and purpose within global teams.

Virtual Leadership and Remote Collaboration: Virtual leadership requires a different set of skills to effectively lead teams spread across different geographical locations. Servant leaders embrace virtual leadership by leveraging technology for remote collaboration, establishing clear communication channels, and providing virtual spaces for team interaction. The emphasis on individual development and relationship-building remains central, even in virtual settings.

Overcoming Time Zone Challenges: Global teams often face the challenge of coordinating work across different time zones. Servant leaders address time zone challenges by implementing flexible working hours, setting clear expectations for communication and deadlines, and utilizing asynchronous communication tools. By recognizing and accommodating time zone differences, leaders ensure that all team members can contribute effectively to shared goals.

Cultural Competence in Virtual Communication: Virtual communication can amplify cultural differences, as non-verbal cues may be limited. Servant leaders prioritize cultural competence in virtual communication by promoting clarity, active listening, and an awareness of cultural nuances. They encourage team members to express their perspectives openly and provide a platform for diverse voices to be heard in virtual discussions.

Building a Unified Team Culture: Building a unified team culture is a central challenge in global teams. Servant leaders foster a sense of unity by emphasizing shared values, goals, and a collective sense of purpose. Regular team meetings, virtual celebrations, and initiatives that highlight the achievements of the entire team contribute to building a unified team culture that transcends geographical boundaries.

Addressing Isolation and Team Cohesion: Team members in global teams may experience feelings of isolation due to physical distance and differences in working hours. Servant leaders address isolation by promoting a culture of inclusivity, facilitating virtual team-building activities, and providing opportunities for social interaction. Cultivating team cohesion, even in virtual environments, contributes to a sense of belonging and shared identity.

Conclusion: Embracing Servant Leadership in a Globalized Digital World

In the globalized and digitally interconnected world of work, servant leadership emerges as a guiding philosophy that transcends cultural boundaries and technological landscapes. The principles of empathy, inclusivity, and a commitment to individual and collective growth provide a solid foundation for leaders navigating the complexities of leading diverse and global teams.

As organizations continue to embrace the opportunities presented by globalization and digitalization, servant leaders stand at the forefront, facilitating collaboration, promoting cultural intelligence, and fostering a sense of unity among team members. The adaptability of servant leadership to different cultural contexts, coupled with its emphasis on individual empowerment and relationship-building, positions it as a powerful approach for leaders striving to navigate the challenges of the globalized digital age.

CHAPTER 13: LEADERSHIP DEVELOPMENT IN A DIGITAL WORLD

13.1 Strategies for Developing Servant Leaders in the Digital Age

The digital age has ushered in a new era of leadership, demanding adaptability, resilience, and a deep understanding of technology. In this landscape, servant leadership principles provide a sturdy foundation for developing leaders who can thrive amidst complexity and uncertainty. This chapter explores strategic approaches for cultivating servant leaders in the digital age, emphasizing the integration of empathy, collaboration, and a commitment to individual and collective growth.

Embedding Servant Leadership in Organizational Culture: Developing servant leaders begins with cultivating a culture that values servant leadership principles.

Organizations must actively embed these principles into their values, mission statements, and leadership expectations. By making servant leadership an integral part of the organizational DNA, leaders at all levels are encouraged to embrace and embody these principles in their daily interactions and decision-making.

Providing Leadership Development Programs: Leadership development programs tailored to the digital age are essential for cultivating servant leaders. These programs should focus on developing skills such as emotional intelligence, effective communication in virtual settings, and adaptability to technological advancements. Interactive workshops, webinars, and virtual coaching sessions can be incorporated to enhance the learning experience and ensure practical application of servant leadership principles.

Promoting Cross-Functional Experiences: Servant leaders benefit from a broad understanding of organizational functions and dynamics. Encouraging cross-functional experiences, where leaders have the opportunity to work in different departments or projects, fosters a holistic perspective. This approach helps leaders develop a deep appreciation for diverse roles within the organization and promotes collaboration across functions.

Incorporating Technology in Leadership Development: The digital age provides a myriad of technological tools that can enhance leadership development. Online learning platforms, virtual reality simulations, and gamified experiences can be integrated into leadership development programs to make learning more engaging and accessible. By leveraging technology, organizations can create dynamic and interactive learning environments that resonate with the digital-savvy leaders of today.

Encouraging Self-Reflection and Feedback: Servant leaders possess a high degree of self-awareness and a commitment to continuous improvement. Leadership development programs should incorporate opportunities for self-reflection and feedback. Virtual platforms can facilitate the collection of feedback from peers, subordinates, and mentors, providing leaders with valuable insights into their strengths and areas for development.

13.2 The Role of Mentorship and Coaching in Virtual Settings

Mentorship and coaching are invaluable components of leadership development, providing personalized guidance and support to aspiring leaders. In the digital age, where virtual interactions are the norm, the role of mentorship and coaching takes on new dimensions. This section explores how organizations can leverage virtual mentorship and coaching to nurture servant leaders.

Establishing Virtual Mentorship Programs: Virtual mentorship programs connect aspiring leaders with experienced mentors, fostering a supportive environment for leadership development. Organizations can facilitate these connections through virtual platforms, ensuring that mentors and mentees can engage in regular video calls, email exchanges, and virtual discussions. The mentorship relationship thrives on mutual respect, open communication, and a shared commitment to personal and professional growth.

Utilizing Technology for Coaching Sessions: Coaching, with its focus on individualized development, is an essential component of leadership growth. In virtual settings, coaching sessions can be conducted through video calls, allowing for face-to-face interactions even when geographically distant. Technology enables the recording of coaching sessions for review, offering leaders the opportunity to revisit insights and recommendations.

Implementing Group Coaching for Team Development:
Group coaching sessions provide a collaborative space for leaders to share experiences, challenges, and insights. In the digital age, these sessions can be conducted through virtual platforms that support group discussions and interactive exercises. Group coaching fosters a sense of community and collective learning, allowing leaders to benefit from diverse perspectives within the group.

Encouraging Reverse Mentoring: In the context of rapid technological advancements, reverse mentoring can be a powerful tool for leadership development. Reverse mentoring involves pairing experienced leaders with younger, tech-savvy individuals who mentor them on digital trends and technologies. This reciprocal learning arrangement enhances the digital fluency of leaders, ensuring they stay informed and adaptive in a rapidly changing technological landscape.

Providing Structured Mentorship and Coaching Programs:
Organizations can formalize mentorship and coaching
programs by establishing structured frameworks. This
includes defining clear goals, expectations, and milestones
for mentorship and coaching relationships. Virtual
platforms can support the implementation of structured
programs, allowing for easy communication, progress
tracking, and resource sharing.

13.3 Continuous Learning and Professional Growth in the Digital Era

Continuous learning is at the heart of leadership
development in the digital era. Servant leaders, committed
to their own growth and the growth of those they lead,
actively seek opportunities for ongoing learning and
professional development. This section explores strategies
for promoting a culture of continuous learning within

organizations, empowering leaders to navigate the ever-evolving digital landscape.

Encouraging a Growth Mindset: A growth mindset is foundational to continuous learning. Organizations can foster a growth mindset culture by promoting the belief that abilities and intelligence can be developed through dedication and hard work. Leaders with a growth mindset embrace challenges, persist in the face of setbacks, and actively seek opportunities to expand their knowledge and skills.

Leveraging Online Learning Platforms: The digital age offers a wealth of online learning platforms that provide access to courses, webinars, and resources on a wide range of topics. Organizations can encourage leaders to leverage these platforms for continuous learning. Subscription-based services, Massive Open Online Courses (MOOCs), and industry-specific platforms offer flexibility and convenience for leaders to engage in self-directed learning.

Implementing Personalized Learning Paths: Recognizing that each leader has unique development needs, organizations can implement personalized learning paths. This involves assessing individual strengths, areas for improvement, and career goals to tailor learning experiences accordingly. Virtual platforms can support the creation and tracking of personalized learning paths, ensuring that leaders receive targeted development opportunities.

Integrating Microlearning for Accessibility: Microlearning, or the delivery of content in small, easily digestible segments, is well-suited to the fast-paced nature of the digital era. Organizations can integrate microlearning into leadership development programs, offering bite-sized lessons that leaders can consume at their own pace. Virtual platforms facilitate the accessibility of microlearning modules, allowing leaders to engage in learning activities as part of their daily routines.

Promoting Knowledge Sharing and Collaboration: Continuous learning is enhanced through knowledge sharing and collaboration. Organizations can establish virtual forums, discussion groups, and collaborative platforms where leaders can share insights, best practices, and resources. These virtual spaces create a community of learners, fostering a culture where knowledge is actively exchanged, and leaders collectively contribute to each other's growth.

Conclusion: Nurturing Servant Leaders in the Digital Era

As organizations navigate the complexities of the digital era, the cultivation of servant leaders becomes not only a strategic imperative but a cornerstone of sustainable success. Through intentional leadership development strategies, the integration of virtual mentorship and coaching, and a commitment to continuous learning, organizations can nurture servant leaders who embody the principles of empathy, collaboration, and a dedication to individual and collective growth.

CHAPTER 14: CASE STUDIES OF SUCCESSFUL DIGITAL SERVANT LEADERSHIP

14.1 Introduction to Digital Servant Leadership Case Studies

In the dynamic landscape of the digital age, organizations are increasingly recognizing the value of servant leadership principles to navigate complexities, foster innovation, and build resilient teams. This chapter explores real-world case studies of organizations that have successfully applied digital servant leadership. Through these examples, we aim to uncover valuable insights, lessons learned, and best practices that illuminate the transformative impact of servant leadership on organizational success in the digital era.

14.2 Case Study 1: Google - Empowering Innovation through Servant Leadership

Background: Google, a global technology giant, is renowned for its innovative culture and disruptive approach to business. Sundar Pichai, the CEO of Google, has been recognized for his adoption of servant leadership principles to empower teams and drive innovation in the rapidly evolving digital landscape.

Application of Servant Leadership: At Google, servant leadership is ingrained in the organizational culture, emphasizing the empowerment of employees and a commitment to serving users worldwide. Sundar Pichai has fostered a culture where leaders prioritize the needs of their teams, provide the autonomy to explore innovative ideas, and create an environment that values continuous learning and collaboration.

Lessons Learned and Best Practices:

1. **Autonomy and Innovation:** Google's success in fostering innovation is attributed to its commitment to providing employees with the autonomy to explore creative solutions. Servant leadership principles, such as empowerment and trust, contribute to a culture where individuals feel encouraged to take risks and experiment with new ideas.

2. **Focus on User-Centricity:** Servant leaders at Google prioritize the needs of users, aligning their strategies with a deep understanding of user experiences. This focus on user-centricity ensures that innovation is driven by a genuine desire to serve and enhance the lives of users, reflecting a core tenet of servant leadership.

3. **Continuous Learning and Development:** Google emphasizes continuous learning and development as

part of its servant leadership philosophy. Leaders actively support the professional growth of their teams through access to learning resources, mentorship programs, and a commitment to creating an environment where curiosity and learning are valued.

4. **Inclusive Decision-Making:** Servant leadership at Google encourages inclusive decision-making, where leaders seek input from diverse perspectives. This approach fosters a collaborative environment where the collective intelligence of the team is harnessed to make informed decisions, aligning with servant leadership principles of collaboration and inclusivity.

Impact on Organizational Success: Google's application of servant leadership has contributed to its status as a global innovation powerhouse. The organization's ability to adapt to technological advancements, drive disruptive changes, and maintain a user-centric focus has been pivotal to its success in the highly competitive tech industry. The impact of servant leadership is evident in Google's sustained growth, employee satisfaction, and its ability to deliver products and services that resonate with users worldwide.

14.3 Case Study 2: Zappos - Cultivating a Servant Leadership Culture for Employee Engagement

Background: Zappos, an online retail company known for its customer-centric approach, has garnered attention for its unique corporate culture. Tony Hsieh, the former CEO of Zappos, was a proponent of servant leadership principles, fostering a workplace culture that prioritizes employee engagement and well-being.

Application of Servant Leadership: Zappos embraced servant leadership by focusing on the happiness and fulfillment of its employees. Tony Hsieh believed that by creating a positive and supportive work environment, employees would, in turn, provide exceptional service to customers. Servant leadership principles at Zappos include active listening, empowerment, and a commitment to creating a workplace where employees feel valued.

Lessons Learned and Best Practices:

1. **Employee-Centric Culture:** Zappos' servant leadership culture places employees at the center of the organization. This is reflected in practices such as eliminating hierarchical structures, providing flexibility in work arrangements, and fostering a sense of community. The emphasis on employee well-being aligns with servant leadership principles of empathy and a commitment to individual growth.

2. **Holacracy and Empowerment:** Zappos embraced holacracy, a non-traditional organizational structure that distributes authority and decision-making. This approach empowers employees to take ownership of

their roles and contribute to the overall success of the organization. Servant leadership, in this context, involves providing the tools and support needed for employees to thrive in a holacratic environment.

3. **Focus on Core Values:** Servant leaders at Zappos emphasize the importance of aligning actions with core values. The organization places a strong emphasis on cultural fit during the hiring process, ensuring that employees resonate with the company's values. This commitment to values-based leadership contributes to a cohesive and engaged workforce.

4. **Investment in Employee Development:** Servant leadership at Zappos includes a commitment to the ongoing development of employees. The organization provides learning opportunities, mentorship programs, and resources to support professional growth. This investment in employee

development aligns with servant leadership
principles of nurturing the potential of individuals.

Impact on Organizational Success: Zappos' application of servant leadership has had a profound impact on its organizational success. The company has been recognized for its exceptional customer service, which is attributed to the positive and engaged culture fostered by servant leadership principles. Zappos' commitment to employee well-being and empowerment has translated into high levels of job satisfaction, low turnover rates, and a strong organizational reputation.

14.4 Case Study 3: IBM - Navigating Digital Transformation with Servant Leadership

Background: IBM, a global technology and consulting company, has undergone significant transformations to adapt to the digital age. Ginni Rometty, the former CEO of IBM, employed servant leadership principles to guide the organization through a period of digital transformation and technological disruption.

Application of Servant Leadership: Ginni Rometty emphasized servant leadership principles as a strategic approach to navigate IBM through digital transformation. The organization prioritized employee empowerment, collaboration, and a focus on customer needs to drive innovation and maintain relevance in the rapidly evolving technology landscape.

Lessons Learned and Best Practices:

1. **Strategic Alignment with Purpose:** IBM's application of servant leadership involves aligning the organization's purpose with its strategies. By emphasizing a commitment to solving complex problems for clients and society, IBM instills a sense of purpose that guides decision-making and innovation. Servant leaders ensure that the

organization's strategies align with its broader mission and values.

2. **Agility and Adaptability:** Digital transformation requires organizations to be agile and adaptable. Servant leadership at IBM involves creating an environment where teams can quickly respond to changing market conditions, technological advancements, and customer needs. This emphasis on agility ensures that the organization remains resilient in the face of digital disruption.

3. **Empowering Employees for Innovation:** IBM places a strong emphasis on empowering employees to contribute to innovation. Servant leaders provide the resources, training, and support needed for employees to embrace a mindset of continuous innovation. This approach aligns with servant leadership principles of empowerment and a

commitment to the growth and development of individuals.

4. **Collaboration Across Disciplines:** Digital transformation often involves breaking down silos and fostering collaboration across different disciplines. IBM's servant leadership culture encourages cross-functional collaboration, ensuring that diverse perspectives and expertise are brought together to address complex challenges. This collaborative approach reflects servant leadership principles of inclusivity and shared decision-making.

Impact on Organizational Success: IBM's application of servant leadership has been instrumental in its ability to navigate digital transformation successfully. The organization has maintained its position as a leader in the technology and consulting industry by adapting to emerging technologies, meeting the evolving needs of clients, and fostering a culture of innovation. The impact of servant leadership is evident in IBM's continued relevance and success in a highly competitive and dynamic market.

14.5 Analyzing the Impact on Organizational Success

Common Themes Across Case Studies:

1. **Empowerment and Autonomy:** Across the case studies, empowerment and autonomy emerge as consistent themes. Servant leaders empower their teams by providing the autonomy to make decisions, take risks, and contribute to the organization's success. This empowerment fosters a culture of ownership and innovation.

2. **Focus on Employee Well-Being:** All the organizations highlighted in the case studies prioritize employee well-being as a core aspect of servant leadership. Whether through unique organizational cultures, flexible work arrangements,

or investment in employee development, servant leaders recognize the importance of creating a positive and supportive workplace.

3. **Commitment to Continuous Learning:**

   Continuous learning is a shared value among servant leadership case studies. Organizations that embrace servant leadership actively promote a culture of continuous learning, providing resources, mentorship, and opportunities for professional development to support the growth of their teams.

4. **Customer-Centric Approach:** Servant leaders consistently adopt a customer-centric approach, aligning organizational strategies with the needs and expectations of customers. This focus on understanding and serving the end-user contributes to the success and sustainability of these organizations in competitive markets.

Impact on Organizational Success: The impact of servant leadership on organizational success is evident in various aspects, including:

1. **Innovation and Adaptability:** Servant leadership fosters a culture of innovation and adaptability, enabling organizations to stay ahead in rapidly evolving industries. The commitment to empowering employees and encouraging continuous learning contributes to the agility needed for successful adaptation to change.

2. **Employee Satisfaction and Retention:** Organizations that prioritize servant leadership principles experience higher levels of employee satisfaction and retention. The positive workplace cultures created by servant leaders contribute to a sense of belonging, purpose, and fulfillment among employees, leading to increased loyalty to the organization.

3. **Resilience in Digital Transformation:** Servant leadership is a key factor in the resilience of organizations undergoing digital transformation. By focusing on empowerment, collaboration, and strategic alignment, servant leaders guide their organizations through complex technological changes, ensuring sustained relevance and success.

4. **Positive Organizational Reputation:** The impact of servant leadership extends to the reputation of organizations. Those known for embracing servant leadership principles often enjoy positive perceptions in the eyes of employees, customers, and the wider community. A positive organizational reputation contributes to long-term success and sustainability.

14.6 Conclusion: Lessons from Successful Digital Servant Leadership

The case studies presented in this chapter offer valuable insights into the application of servant leadership principles in the digital age. Across diverse industries and organizational contexts, common themes of empowerment, employee well-being, continuous learning, and a customer-centric focus emerge as foundational elements of successful digital servant leadership.

As organizations continue to navigate the complexities of the digital era, the lessons learned from these case studies provide a roadmap for leaders seeking to embrace servant leadership principles. The transformative impact of servant leadership on organizational success is not only evident in financial metrics but also in the creation of positive workplace cultures, the ability to foster innovation, and the resilience to thrive in dynamic and competitive environments.

CHAPTER 15: CONCLUSION

15.1 Recap of Key Points

In this journey through the pages of "Servant Leadership in the Digital Age," we have explored the transformative power of servant leadership principles in navigating the complexities of the evolving digital landscape. Let's take a moment to recap the key points that have unfolded throughout this exploration.

Understanding the Digital Age and Servant Leadership: We began our journey with an overview of the digital age, acknowledging its profound impact on leadership dynamics. The emergence of digital technologies, globalization, and the shift in paradigms necessitate a new approach to leadership. Introducing servant leadership principles, we recognized the significance of authenticity and relationship-building in virtual and globalized work environments.

The Evolution of Leadership in the Digital Era: Delving into the historical perspective of leadership, we traced the evolution of leadership styles in the context of digital advancements. The shifting paradigms in the digital era highlighted the need for adaptive and inclusive leadership approaches, laying the groundwork for the exploration of servant leadership.

Understanding Servant Leadership: Chapter 3 brought us to the heart of servant leadership, defining its principles and exploring its historical roots. The relevance of servant leadership in contemporary contexts became apparent, setting the stage for a deeper dive into its application in the digital age.

Digital Challenges in Leadership: Identifying the challenges posed by digital advancements, Chapter 4 prompted a reflection on the complexities of leading in a globalized and technologically driven environment. The need for balance between innovation and stability became a focal point, emphasizing the role of servant leadership in navigating these challenges.

Authenticity in the Digital Age: Chapter 5 delved into the importance of authenticity in the digital age, recognizing both the challenges and opportunities it presents. Building trust in virtual relationships emerged as a critical aspect, reinforcing the authentic leadership values inherent in servant leadership.

Building Relationships in a Virtual World: Strategies for effective relationship-building in digital spaces took center stage in Chapter 6. Overcoming communication barriers in virtual teams and fostering a sense of community in remote work environments were explored as integral components of servant leadership in the digital era.

Servant Leadership and Team Dynamics: Applying servant leadership principles to team dynamics was the focus of Chapter 7. Empowering and developing team members in a digital setting and cultivating a culture of collaboration and shared goals were identified as key strategies for servant leaders.

Emotional Intelligence in Digital Leadership: Chapter 8 emphasized the role of emotional intelligence in leadership, exploring how it can be recognized and managed in virtual teams. Enhancing interpersonal skills in the digital workplace emerged as a vital aspect of servant leadership.

Navigating Change in the Digital Landscape: Adapting servant leadership to guide teams through digital transformation became the focus of Chapter 9. Strategies for leading change in a dynamic environment and overcoming resistance to digital change were explored, highlighting the adaptability inherent in servant leadership.

The Ethics of Digital Leadership: Chapter 10 delved into ethical considerations in the digital age, emphasizing the delicate balance between innovation and ethical decision-making. The impact of digital leadership on organizational values underscored the ethical dimension inherent in servant leadership.

Innovation and Creativity in Servant Leadership: Fostering innovation through servant leadership principles was explored in Chapter 11. Encouraging creativity in a digital workplace and leveraging technology for organizational growth showcased the role of servant leaders as catalysts for innovation.

Servant Leadership in Globalized Work Environments: Leading diverse and multicultural teams took the spotlight in Chapter 12. Adapting servant leadership to different cultural contexts and addressing the challenges of leading global teams in the digital age were central themes, highlighting the universal applicability of servant leadership.

Leadership Development in a Digital World: Chapter 13 unfolded strategies for developing servant leaders in the digital age. The role of mentorship and coaching in virtual settings, along with a focus on continuous learning and professional growth, underscored the dynamic nature of leadership development in the digital era.

Case Studies of Successful Digital Servant Leadership: Chapter 14 provided real-world examples of organizations applying servant leadership principles. The case studies of Google, Zappos, and IBM illuminated the impact of servant leadership on innovation, employee engagement, and organizational success in diverse contexts.

15.2 The Future of Servant Leadership in the Evolving Digital Landscape

As we stand at the intersection of servant leadership and the evolving digital landscape, it is imperative to contemplate the future trajectory of leadership. The principles of servant leadership, with their emphasis on empathy, collaboration, and individual growth, align seamlessly with the needs of the digital age.

Adapting to Technological Advancements: The future of servant leadership involves a continuous adaptation to technological advancements. As digital tools and artificial intelligence become increasingly integrated into the workplace, servant leaders must leverage these technologies to enhance communication, foster collaboration, and facilitate learning.

Navigating Virtual Workspaces: Virtual workspaces are likely to become more prevalent, requiring leaders to excel in leading remote and global teams. The principles of servant leadership, such as building authentic relationships, fostering a sense of community, and promoting inclusivity, will play a pivotal role in creating cohesive virtual teams.

Embracing Diversity and Inclusion: The digital era has facilitated global connectivity, making diversity and inclusion more critical than ever. Servant leaders will need to embrace diverse perspectives, adapt their leadership styles to different cultural contexts, and champion inclusivity to build high-performing and harmonious teams.

Ethical Leadership in the Digital Age: Ethical considerations in the digital age will continue to be a central theme. Servant leaders, committed to values-based decision-making, will be at the forefront of guiding organizations through ethical challenges, ensuring that innovation is balanced with a strong ethical foundation.

Leadership Development in a Dynamic Landscape: The landscape of leadership development will evolve in response to the changing demands of the digital era. Servant leadership will continue to be a guiding philosophy, emphasizing personalized development, virtual mentorship, and a commitment to continuous learning as leaders navigate the complexities of the digital world.

15.3 Call to Action: Embracing Servant Leadership Principles in the Digital Age

As we conclude this exploration of servant leadership in the digital age, the call to action is clear: Leaders must embrace servant leadership principles to thrive in the evolving landscape. The transformative impact of servant leadership is not a theoretical concept but a practical and actionable approach to leadership excellence.

Prioritize Authenticity and Relationship-Building: In the digital age, where virtual interactions can sometimes feel disconnected, leaders must prioritize authenticity. Authentic leadership builds trust, fosters genuine connections, and cultivates a positive organizational culture. Embrace open communication, share your values transparently, and prioritize relationship-building in both virtual and physical spaces.

Empower and Develop Your Team: Servant leaders recognize the potential within each team member and actively work to empower and develop them. Encourage autonomy, provide opportunities for skill development, and foster a culture where individual growth is not just encouraged but celebrated. By investing in your team, you contribute to the collective success of the organization.

Embrace a Global and Inclusive Mindset: The digital age has made the world more interconnected than ever before. Leaders must embrace a global and inclusive mindset, appreciating the diversity of perspectives and cultural backgrounds within their teams. Actively seek out opportunities to learn about different cultures, adapt your leadership style to different contexts, and create an environment where every voice is valued.

Navigate Change with Resilience and Adaptability: Change is a constant in the digital age, and leaders must navigate it with resilience and adaptability. Servant leaders excel in guiding their teams through change by providing a clear sense of purpose, involving team members in decision-making, and fostering a culture of agility. Embrace change as an opportunity for growth and innovation.

Champion Ethics and Values: In a landscape where technological advancements can sometimes outpace ethical considerations, leaders must champion ethics and values. Ensure that your decisions align with the core values of the organization, and actively consider the ethical implications of technological innovations. By prioritizing ethics, you contribute to the long-term sustainability and reputation of your organization.

Invest in Continuous Learning and Development: The digital age demands continuous learning and adaptability. Leaders should invest in their own continuous learning journey and create a culture of learning within their teams. Leverage online platforms, mentorship programs, and other resources to stay abreast of industry trends and equip your team with the skills needed for success.

Celebrate Innovation and Creativity: Servant leaders foster a culture of innovation and creativity. Encourage your team to think creatively, experiment with new ideas, and embrace a mindset of continuous improvement. Leverage technology to drive innovation and position your organization at the forefront of industry advancements.

Lead with Emotional Intelligence: Emotional intelligence is a cornerstone of servant leadership. Cultivate self-awareness, recognize and manage emotions in yourself and others, and prioritize empathy in your leadership approach. In the digital workplace, where virtual interactions can sometimes lack nuance, emotional intelligence becomes even more crucial for effective leadership.

Promote a Positive Organizational Culture: Servant leaders actively contribute to creating a positive organizational culture. Foster a culture of collaboration, appreciation, and mutual support. Recognize and celebrate achievements, no matter how small, and actively work to mitigate negativity or toxicity within the team. A positive culture is the bedrock of sustained success.

15.4 The Journey Continues: Applying Servant Leadership in Your Context

As we conclude this exploration of servant leadership in the digital age, the journey continues in your hands. The principles and insights shared in these pages serve as a guide, but it is through your actions and commitment that the true impact of servant leadership will be realized in your organizational context.

Whether you lead a small team, an entire department, or an organization, the application of servant leadership principles can foster positive change. As you navigate the complexities of the digital age, keep in mind the core tenets of authenticity, empathy, empowerment, and a commitment to continuous growth.

The journey of servant leadership is not a solitary one; it is a collective effort that involves every member of the organization. Engage your team in the dialogue, seek their input, and encourage a shared commitment to the principles of servant leadership. The collaborative spirit inherent in servant leadership aligns seamlessly with the interconnected nature of the digital age.

Remember that servant leadership is not a one-size-fits-all solution; it is a flexible and adaptable philosophy that can be tailored to your unique organizational context. Embrace the principles that resonate most strongly with your values and the needs of your team, and be open to continuous refinement as you learn and grow.

As you embark on the journey of applying servant leadership in your context, reflect on the lessons learned from the case studies, the strategies for leadership development, and the insights shared by leaders who have successfully navigated the digital landscape. Embrace the challenges as opportunities for growth, and celebrate the successes as milestones in your journey toward leadership excellence.

15.5 A Gratitude for the Journey

Before we part ways, let me express my gratitude for accompanying you on this exploration of servant leadership in the digital age. The commitment to leadership excellence and the desire to foster positive change within your sphere of influence are admirable qualities that will undoubtedly shape the future of leadership in the digital era.

As you carry the principles of servant leadership into your professional journey, remember that leadership is not a destination but a continuous evolution. Stay curious, stay empathetic, and stay committed to the principles that resonate with your leadership philosophy.

May your journey be filled with meaningful connections, transformative insights, and the satisfaction of knowing that your leadership contributes to the positive growth of individuals and organizations alike. As the digital landscape continues to evolve, may you navigate it with resilience, adaptability, and the unwavering commitment to servant leadership.

The future of leadership is in your hands, and I am confident that, armed with the principles of servant leadership, you will not only navigate the complexities of the digital age but also inspire positive change in those you lead.

Safe travels on your leadership journey and may the principles of servant leadership guide you to new heights of success and fulfillment.

With gratitude,

Dr. Shaun Nichols

www.ingramcontent.com/pod-product-compliance
Lightning Source LLC
Chambersburg PA
CBHW072209290526

45794CB00004B/1702